The Ogders
of No 13

The Ogdens of No 13

DARAN LITTLE

BOXTREE

Published in association with

GRANADA TELEVISION

Published in association with Granada Television

ACKNOWLEDGEMENTS
The publishers would like to thank the following for their help in organising all the pictures for this book:

Kathryn de Belle, Alan Smyllie, Jim Rowan, David Collins, Tom Purslow and Ian Cartwright.

This book is dedicated to Jacqui Hayden.

First published in 1992 by Boxtree Limited

10 9 8 7 6 5 4 3 2 1

Editing and additional writing: Mary Lambert
Design: Penny Mills
Jacket design: Paterson-Jones
Printed and bound in Italy through OFSA

BOXTREE LIMITED
36 Tavistock Street
London WC2E 7PB

ISBN 1-85283-178-2

Contents

Introduction

'The Ogden's! The only good thing I can say about them is that they'd spoil another couple, they were made for each other. God 'elp 'em!'

Elsie Tanner

When Stan and Hilda Ogden moved into Number 13 Coronation Street in June 1964 they had been married for 21 years. They had met during World War 2 in the blackout when Hilda had tripped over a drunken Stan. They were married in a few days, but the bliss of their wedding night was spoilt the next morning when Stan was arrested by the military police for overstaying his leave. This was the first of the many ups and downs in their turbulent marriage.

Back from the War, Stan became a long-distance lorry driver and spent weeks away from home. Hilda hardly heard from him, she received little money, and struggled to keep a roof over the heads of their four children: Freda (later Irma), Dudley (later Trevor), Tony and Sylvia. The two youngest children, Tony and Sylvia, were mentally retarded and were placed in a home as Hilda couldn't cope. Hilda's life became complete when they moved into Number 13 Coronation Street – the family's first real home.

Hilda and Stan's marriage was not made in heaven. There were frequent arguments when Stan was drunk and Hilda often suffered the back of his hand, but they also had some good laughs. People were amused by the Laurel and Hardy couple - Stan with his large beer belly and Hilda with her sparrow-like frame. Many a time they would be seen at the Rovers Return pub with Stan silently drinking at the bar while Hilda nagged him about another of his failed money earning schemes. Stan even got the nickname of 'Workshy Oggie' because of his lazy attitude to work, prompting Hilda to say to him once: 'Lax - that's your failing. Lax from the neck up and relax from the neck down'.

Against all odds the Ogdens survived 40 years of marriage. Behind their comic repartee lay a trust and understanding in each other. Separately they were two of life's victims, together they were an invincible force. Hilda once joked with Stan: 'If there's a lack of mutual trust in this marriage there's an even bigger lack of mutual money! Trust grows as the length of your purse grows'.

Hilda and Stan had a turbulent marriage for 40 years with frequent disagreements and arguments, but they were also great pals and each had the ability to make each other laugh

Happy Families

'Get it into yer head woman. Lousy husband, lousy son, lousy daughter, that's all you've bloomin' got!'

Stan Ogden to Hilda Ogden

After frequently moving homes, the Ogdens bought Number 13 Coronation Street and were united together again as a family

At the time of their move to Number 13 Coronation Street in June 1964, Stan and Hilda Ogden had been married for 21 years. For most of that time Stan had worked away from home and left Hilda to bring up their children – Irma, Trevor, Tony and Sylvia – singlehandedly. The family never stayed in one place for long and often left under the cover of darkness to avoid paying the landlord.

The Ogdens moved to Coronation Street in an attempt to

rebuild their disintegrating marriage, Hilda had threatened to leave Stan if he didn't give up his job as a lorry driver and come home for good. She had been unable to support all the family and when she was told that the two youngest children, Tony and Sylvia, were mentally retarded she was relieved when they were placed in a special home.

Irma was the first Ogden to go down Coronation Street. She'd left school at 15 and joined the staff at Elliston's Raincoat Factory which backed onto the Street. She left home in 1963 at 17, after another row with Hilda about an unsuitable boyfriend. She moved into a flat over a pie shop with barmaid Marion Black, and to make her sound more glamorous she changed her name from Freda to Irma.

When Stan Ogden gave up driving lorries he promised Hilda that all the family would live together again. He tracked his daughter down to the Street in June 1964, but he had problems finding her at first as everyone knew her as Irma and not Freda. Irma had not seen her father for six years; his job as a long distance lorry driver had ensured his prolonged absence. During that time she had watched her mother Hilda struggle with looking after the children whilst Stan sent virtually no earnings home. Hilda had supported the family by doing cleaning work and taking in a bit of washing. Irma did not believe her father when he told her he wanted her to come home and said bitterly: 'Prove it. If you're really serious about gettin' a place for us to live, there's a house for sale in this street, Number 13. Buy it'.

Irma

Hilda and Stan's daughter, Freda, left home at 15 and changed her name to Irma. Stan tracked her down in June 1964 and she agreed to come home, providing he bought a house – Number 13

Irma moves back

Irma finally moved back with her parents, but to escape their rows (above right) *she worked at the Corner Shop* (above) *and in the evenings at the Rovers Return* (top)

Stan was forced to admit he'd managed to save £200 from his lorry driving wages and this was used as a deposit on Number 13. They managed to get a mortgage on the balance and because the house was empty the transaction was quickly completed and a week later the Ogdens moved in. Although Stan and Hilda were reconciled they still constantly argued and Irma spent most of her time escaping to her new job at the Corner Shop or to work in the evenings at the Rovers bar. She bitterly regretted her loss of independence.

Irma first started going out with David Barlow, a professional second-division footballer, when he came up from London to stay with his brother for Christmas in 1964. Although she really liked David she felt embarrassed by his extravagance with money and she always felt out of place at his favourite jazz club. He did not like her working as a barmaid, telling her it was a common job. She refused to change and become more sophisticated just to suit him and angrily retorted: 'Well I'll tell you summat – that's me too. Cheap an' common. if you don't like me the way I am, it's just too bad. I'm me, see – an' you either put up with me or find someone else!'

David realised how much he cared for Irma and proposed to her during the Street's outing to the Blue John mines in the spring of 1965. Her parents were delighted that she'd made such a good match, but David's educated brother Ken was horrified. The idea of being related by marriage to the unsophisticated Ogden family was just too much to bear. David thought he was being pompous and teased him: 'Come off it Ken. You're the same as the Ogdens underneath and you know it. You were born 'ere – Coronation Street – a two up an' two down terraced with a backyard an' an outside lavatory. Our Dad was a postman

David Barlow

David started taking Irma out in early 1965. After she refused to change her ways (top) he fell in love with her spirited personality. He proposed to her (above) on a street outing in the spring of 1965

11

Marriage December 18th 1965

Irma's plans for a quiet, secret wedding (right) were spoilt when her parents and neighbours discovered where they were and gatecrashed the reception (above)

an' our Mam was a cleaner in a hotel. Not much to be proud in that is there?'

David had £1,180 saved and Irma looked forward to getting married quickly and buying a property in Cheshire. Their families wanted a white wedding but David and Irma wanted to save their money and they secretly eloped to Rideway Street Registry Office on December 18th 1965 with two of David's footballer friends as witnesses. Their taxi driver gossiped to some neighbours about the couple and the Street's residents gatecrashed the reception. David and Irma bought a house in Sandy Lane, Oakhill and looked forward to their future life together. They had only been married for two weeks when David had a bad football accident and was told he could never play again. Irma persuaded him to consider running a business and they took over the Corner Shop in February 1966.

Trade at the shop was a bit slow and to help with their finances, Irma took a part-time job as a plastic welder at Elliston's leaving David to cope on his own. She hated it, as she was given the most difficult machine to use by the foreman and kept burning the plastic. The couple both wanted children and Irma left the factory to try for a family. She was even more convinced when she swapped places for a day with her sister-in-law, Valerie Barlow and looked after her twin babies. It didn't take Irma long to get pregnant, but sadly two months later in November 1967 she miscarried. Although the doctors told her there would be no problem in having another baby Irma refused to believe them and said to David: 'It's bound to 'appen again. Just because I'm scared it will. You shouldn't need kids!'

Shortly after buying the Corner Shop in 1966, Irma delightedly announced that she was pregnant. The Barlow's joy did not last long as she later miscarried

Move to Australia

Hilda's plans to start a new life with the Barlow's in Australia (top) *were ruined by Stan's refusal to leave England. Together they saw Irma off in April 1968* (below)

David was worried about Irma and to help her come to terms with the miscarriage, he suggested that they should foster a child over Christmas 1967. They both enjoyed looking after 12 year-old Jill Morris, who was a happy, easy going child. Irma saw what a good father David would make and felt ready to try for another baby.

David still missed playing football and joined a game one day without telling Irma. He felt no pain in his leg and after consulting a specialist he was told he could play professionally again. An offer came from a team in Australia and attracted by a life in the sun, he readily signed up. Irma was frightened at the thought of living so far away and tried to use the news that she was pregnant again to make emigration impossible. She changed her mind when she saw photographs of the large house in Sydney which accompanied the offer, and the couple left England in April 1968 to start their new life on the other side of the world.

Irma found it hard to adjust to a new country and couldn't cope with the busy, extravagant lifestyle that top footballers were supposed to lead. David loved being out and spent more and more time with his new footballing friends. Even the birth of their son Darren in November 1968 did not help to strengthen the Barlows' weakening marriage. Irma had help with the baby and gradually became more bored with so much time on her own at home. She constantly nagged David who got drunk to blank out her voice. On April 11 1970, David and Irma were having another row as he drove to the coast. Distracted by anger for a few seconds David did not see a lorry pulling out and crashed into it; he was killed instantly and young Darren died later in hospital.

The news of the Barlows' deaths in Australia shocked Coronation Street and Dave Smith lent Hilda some money to fly out and bring Irma home. Battling hard to come to terms with being a widow, Irma kept reproaching herself and admitted to Ken Barlow that she had found it hard to cope with being a famous footballer's wife and had made David's life a misery by nagging him. On hearing this admission Ken angrily replied: 'You can only live for yourself. Because that's all you're capable of. Believe me, when you got married, I thought you were wrong for Dave. But it goes far deeper than than, now I know. You'd be wrong for anybody! If you have to spend the rest of

A tragic end

The neighbours helped Hilda prepare for her trip to Australia after David and Darren's tragic deaths (bottom). *She only stayed long enough to bury David before bringing Irma back home to England* (below)

Irma stole little Anthony Lock from outside the post office in the summer of 1970, thinking he was her dead child, Darren. Her flatmate, Bet Lynch, covered up for her and safely returned the boy to his mother

your life alone, then that's the best way for you, it's the only way you know how! You've got two graves to prove it. That brands you Irma. That brands you for life!'

Feeling sorry for Irma, the local newspaper raised the £600 for Hilda to repay Dave Smith but before she could give it back, Stan used the money to buy Irma a partnership in the corner shop with its new owner Maggie Clegg. Irma moved into the flat above the shop, sharing with Bet Lynch, to get away from Hilda's suffocating mothering. Bet helped her come to terms with Darren's death and returned a baby boy that Irma had stolen from outside the post office, believing it was Darren and that he was still alive.

I rma was determined to look to the future and only two months after David's death she shocked everybody by going out with bookie Dave Smith. She enjoyed his company and convinced Hilda and Stan that they were going to get married. They started to like the idea of having another wealthy son-in-law, but Dave soon informed them *they'd* have to pay for the wedding.

A few months later, Irma met up with American deserter Joe Donnelli. He got drunk one night and tried to force Irma to go to bed with him. When she resisted him he threatened her with violence, admitting to her that he'd murdered Steve Tanner two years previously.

For the next two weeks Irma was terrified and lived in fear of seeing Joe. She swore that she wouldn't tell anyone about his

Joe Donnelli

Joe Donnelli had a disturbed, violent personality and threatened to kill Irma if she told anyone he'd murdered Steve Tanner. He often held her captive in her flat before taking Stan as a hostage at Number 5 on Christmas Eve 1970 (left)

confession but he refused to leave her alone. At night he would wait around the shop until he saw Maggie going out and then he would force his way into the flat and frighten her. Everybody realised something was wrong because of Irma's strange behaviour. Her easy going personality changed; she no longer laughed and joked and appeared jumpy all the time. Finally she told Joe's friend Gregg Flint about his confession. Gregg informed the authorities but Joe escaped and sought refuge with his landlady, Minnie Caldwell and held her at gun point. Stan was shocked when Irma explained how Joe had threatened to stab her with scissors, and unaware that Joe was armed, he broke into Number 5 to confront him. Joe released Minnie but turned the gun on Stan, forcing him to sing carols as it was Christmas Eve. Stan was halfway through the chorus of 'Silent Night' when Joe shot himself.

Emotionally scarred by her experiences with David and Joe, Irma couldn't face going out with men for some months. When she met Eddie Duncan, another professional footballer, she refused to get involved with him. But Eddie was very attractive and had plenty of charm and Irma eventually agreed to a night out. She was older now and had begun to appreciate the glamorous social life of a celebrity. She enjoyed the all-night parties and noisy drinking sessions, but too many late nights began to affect Eddie's performance on the pitch and Dave Smith, part owner of Eddie's club, County, warned Irma that she was ruining Eddie's career. Irma agreed to cool their relationship; Eddie, however, refused to listen to Dave and when Irma refused to go out with him he turned to Bet Lynch for comfort. The sight of Eddie taking Bet out was too much for Irma. She packed and left the Street that same night under the cover of darkness, not even telling Hilda and Stan.

The Ogdens only heard from their daughter occasionally after that. She settled in Llandudno and when Stan died several years later she wrote to Hilda from her new home in Canada, to say how sorry she was.

Eddie Duncan

As the main football star of Coronation Street, Eddie saw his fans turn against him as his game suffered due to his absorbing romance with Irma in 1971

18

The Ogdens' son Trevor did not stay long at Number 13 after their move in 1964. He turned down an apprenticeship with Len Fairclough a few months later and disappeared to London with money stolen from the neighbours' houses while they were all sheltering in the Mission Hall during a bomb scare. Hilda couldn't cope with the fact that her son was a thief and mortified she shouted at Stan: 'You were on the lorries, away more then ye were 'ere. Boys need a father. You'd come back dog tired, boozed up. They you started clattering me about. What he got was pots flyin' about and seein' me with bruises on me face'.

Trevor

Hilda and Stan did not know where they had gone wrong when their intelligent son, Trevor, absconded to London with money he had stolen from their neighbours

Not a word was heard from Trevor for nine years, and in 1973 Hilda tracked him down to Chesterfield where he worked as a rather suspect mortgage broker. He lived in a detached house with wife Polly and son Damien. Hilda was thrilled to find she was a grandmother but Stan soon fell out with Trevor, and they had furious arguments which brought all their anguished differences right to the surface. Bitterly Stan said to Hilda: 'Nine years since he walked out of this house. Nine flamin' years. An' for all he flamin' cares we could both 'ave been dead an' buried by now'.

Trevor kept in touch with his parents to please Polly, and Hilda was allowed to be present at the birth of their

When the Ogdens finally tracked Trevor down in 1973 after nine years (above), *they were thrilled to discover they had a grandson, Damien* (top)

20

daughter Jayne in 1976. He only visited Coronation Street when he needed something, usually money. Although outwardly well off he only rented his house and was always trying to acquire more possessions. The only real interest he showed in his mother was when she was left money in her brother's will. When Stan died in November 1984, Trevor comforted Hilda but made the most of the fact that Irma had not returned from Canada for the funeral.

Trevor and Damien's occasional visits to Number 13 delighted Hilda, but always caused Stan to question his son's motives knowing that he was normally after money

When Hilda left the Street in 1987, she hoped to live with one of her children, watching her grandchildren grow up. She could never understand why they resented their unsettled upbringing; she thought her married life with Stan was how every couple lived. She probably sees Trevor occasionally, when he's in trouble or when Polly forces him, and gets the odd letter from Irma. But the warmth and love that Hilda expected from her children was not to be.

A Marriage of Trust

"'E's a devil for scrappin' is my Stanley. I wish I'd a pound for every crack 'e's given me. I know 'e doesn't mean it. I love him. There's plenty worse then my Stan. I like a man with a bit 'o go in 'm. It's 'armless enough int' it.'

Hilda Ogden to Annie Walker

Hilda and Stan Ogden did not have a conventional marriage. Theirs was a tempestuous, often violent relationship with Hilda's spiteful tongue equalling the strength of Stan's hard hand. For much of their married life Stan was away working as a lorry driver, and Hilda was left alone for long periods to cope on her own with the children. But despite all the rows and differences that peppered their married life they always had a close affectionate bond, and even when they parted on various occasions, they knew they would end up together again.

Annie Walker, Hilda's employer at the Rovers Return, was appalled at the news that Stan regularly beat up Hilda

Shortly after moving into Number 13 Coronation Street in June 1964, Hilda confided in Annie Walker, her employer at the Rovers Return, that Stan regularly hit her. Annie was astounded that Hilda put up with this rough treatment, but Hilda confessed to almost enjoying it as she felt it was Stan's way of showing he loved her. Hilda matched Stan's aggression with her sharp tongue and always gave him back as good as she got.

The Ogdens' marriage survived 40 years of turbulent rows. During that time both were tempted into relationships outside the marriage. Although never really unfaithful to Stan herself, Hilda did not mind if Stan strayed a little as she always knew he would return to her. She had learnt to tolerate the fact that he was useless around the house, bone idle and only worked because she forced him to. When he really annoyed her, she would often mutter to herself, 'No other woman would 'ave you!' Once Stan pushed her too far when a few years later he didn't come home one night. He had been giving Elsie Tanner a driving lesson in her car and they'd run out of petrol. Stranded on the moors they'd had to spend the night there together.

Ups and downs

Stan's physical violence with Hilda was matched by her sharp tongue and even though she constantly nagged and criticised him, he was always willing to show his love for her. He threw a 25th wedding anniversary party for her in 1968

THANKS OUR HILDA FOR 25 GRAND YEARS. 1943–1968

Hilda's breakdown

Stan was confused by Hilda's vague manner (below). *The doctor diagnosed a breakdown and told Stan to give her much support* (bottom)

Hilda believed Stan's story that they had whiled away the hours playing childhood games but felt it was a matter of pride to have it out in public with her old enemy and neighbour, the glamorous Elsie Tanner. Elsie found Hilda's jealousy very amusing, but couldn't wait to put her straight by answering back: 'I may be getting desperate Mrs Ogden, but I'm not so desperate that I have to scrape the bottom of't barrel...and no other feller would ever look at you twice!'

After a period of overwork and continual fighting with Elsie Tanner, who Stan had admitted he found attractive, Hilda began to feel very down in the summer of 1967. Life in the crowded Street was just not very appealing any more. The first signs that it was a nervous breakdown rather than bad depression was when Hilda neglected her household jobs to go and watch the ducks in the park. Her memory became vague, she forgot to make Stan's tea and was found walking around the Street in her slippers. She felt her life was empty and lacked beauty and was once heard to say: 'I've never seen a butterfly in t'backyard. I don't know what I want out 'o life. It used to be just 'aving Stan

in work. Hopin' I weren't lookin' any older. An' a short fur jacket. I always wanted a short fur jacket. Now I don't know so much. I wouldn't mind just summat to look forward to. Summat nice to 'appen. But that's talkin' daft, in't it?'

Stan did not understand what was happening at first and began to feel annoyed that he had to cook his own meals. When Hilda disappeared with the club outing money, which he held as treasurer, he presumed she'd gone off with another man. Stan and daughter Irma both covered up for Hilda during her absence, but it was a week before she was brought home in a sedated state by a doctor after being found wandering on the Pier head in Liverpool. The doctor told Stan that Hilda was subconsciously jealous of Elsie Tanner's marriage to the American, Steve Tanner, and diagnosed paranoid psychosis. Stan rallied round for once and gave her the support and love she needed to get better.

As part of her recovery in the following months Hilda went for regular walks in the park and often chatted to park keeper, George Greenwood. They used to sit in his little hut and Hilda would tell him about all her hopes and aspirations in life. When he gave her a budgie called Mabel, she was deeply touched and left it in the hut with George's own budgie, Winston, to keep him company.

Unknown to Hilda, George's wife Agnes found out about their meetings and called on Stan and begged him not to

Hilda was delighted when her friend, George Greenwood, presented her with a pet of her own, a budgie called Mabel

George Greenwood

Agnes, George's wife, visited Stan and explained the advantages of George and Hilda's affair (top). Hilda felt too guilty to go on seeing George (above) in early 1968

stop the liaision, saying: 'I wouldn't know what to do with meself if he changed, It's allus round Jan, Feb. Quiet time in his trade, y'see. There's allus some lonely soul, 'e meets 'er regular for a month or so...then he comes all over guilty. 'Cose in 'is mind he's wronged me. An' that upsets 'im somethin' shockin'. E's a man wi' a very strong conscience, is George. So 'e tries to make it up t'me. I get more fussin', more presents, more attention in Jan an' Feb than I get all't rest o't year out together. An' if you play yer cards right, you'll be treated same way'.

When Hilda met widower George again in 1971, she found the strong attraction they had felt for each other had died

Hilda soon grew guilty about her little 'affair' and wrote Stan a note telling him all about George. Stan ignored it as he was happy receiving all the extra attention Hilda was giving him. She cooked more expensive meals and kept slipping him some extra beer money. The relationship was finished by Hilda after only a few weeks when she discovered that Stan had been seen with another woman – Agnes. She left George her budgie Mabel so that he could always be reminded of her.

They met up again a few years later when George, now a widower, came to the Street to judge a flower show. Hilda was thrilled to see George and dressed up specially for him, but although he was pleased to see her it was obvious that he was no longer interested in her. Stan took advantage of the situation to enter an orchid he had stolen from the park in the show. George immediately recognised the flower and upset Hilda by deriding Stan's childish tactics in front of her.

Stan's relationship with Clara Regan was the standing joke of the neighbourhood. She had been married three times and lived at Number 19 Inkerman Street. Stan met her on his window cleaning round in 1968. In his usual clumsy way he had put his foot through her fan light and repaired it for her. Stan took a fancy to Clara and called in for cups of tea on his round. The nosy neighbours soon called her 'Stan's bit on the side' but Hilda after meeting her was convinced that Stan remained faithful and said to a friend: 'If I really thought Inkerman Street or 'owt else were givin' me Stan the itch I know what I's do, what yer do with any itch. Yer flamin' well scratch it'.

His regular visits were abruptly stopped by Clara a few years later, and people started gossiping saying that it was

Clara Regan

Gossip that Stan was co-habiting with Clara Regan infuriated Hilda (top) as she knew it was untrue. Stan's ego was badly deflated when Hilda firmly stated that no other woman would even bother to take a second look at him (below)

because the Social Security office thought Stan was living with Mrs Regan. Appalled that he might be interviewed by them Stan turned to Hilda for help. She went round to see Clara and found out that she had a man living with her. Smugly she gave Stan the news and assured him in her usual blunt and sarcastic tones: 'I mean the train goin' through a tunnel noise I hear in mi lughole every night. That's you, isn't it? And I'd know if you got up in middle o' night and went and slapped yer cold feet on her in Inkerman Street, wouldn't I? In future if yer cart should accidently turn int' Inkerman Street. All by i'self of course. I'd be firm and stop i' dead in its tracks. In other words keep away. Or I'll play a tune on yer head with a cobbler's last'.

As the years passed Stan and Hilda began to think about planning for their retirement. They tried to think of various schemes to give them some extra money and hit upon the idea of selling their house and running the Community Centre as caretakers. They thought the position would really suit them and Hilda said to Stan: 'It's a nice place, the Centre. We could 'ave Trevor and Polly come t'see us – and not be ashamed'.

When Hilda resigned from her cleaning job at the Rovers Return Annie Walker gave her the best reference she felt she could: 'To whom it may concern. Since Mrs Ogden joined my staff her conduct has been all I have come to expect of her. Her spirit of cooperation is out of the ordinary. Her attendance and her application to work are entirely consistent with her other aptitudes. Her interest in other people is unique to herself and I can unreservedly recommend her for any post requiring an involvement in the affairs of the people around her. Should Mrs Ogden be successful in obtaining another post, I cannot say how sorry I shall be to lose her. But I can say in truth that Mrs Ogden will leave a gap at the Rovers Return which I am quite sure no one else will be able to fill'.

Unfortunately three of the Centre's committee members, Alf Roberts and the Bishop's, couldn't bear the thought of working with Stan and voted against the Ogdens becoming caretakers. Gertie Robson was appointed in their place in July 1974 but gave up the job a few months later and the committee finally

Stan and Hilda looked forward to the future in June 1974 as they happily applied for the secure caretaking at at the Community Centre

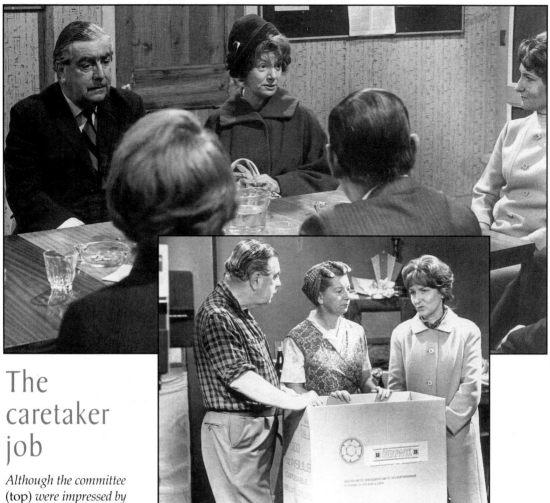

The caretaker job

Although the committee (top) were impressed by Hilda's glowing reference from Annie Walker, they were forced to turn the Ogdens down because of their record with the Health Department (right)

offered the Ogdens the position. They sold Number 13 for £2,500 and looked forward to a wealthier more secure, future. It was not to be, and at the last moment the offer was retracted because the committee found out about the Ogdens' record with the Public Health department. In the previous twelve months the Health Inspector had called at Number 13 because of mice infestation and Stan had been reported for keeping a donkey in the back yard. Reluctantly the Ogdens stopped the sale on their home and stayed on in the Street.

For the next few years Hilda and Stan were content to stay on in their home, but that all changed when Hilda went to nurse her sick brother Archie in his new,

stylish home. Hilda fell in love with a modern house valued at £17,000 on the nearby River Park Estate. Ignoring Stan's protests she put their house on the market for £7,000 and planned to take a mortgage out on the outstanding amount, based on their income and the rent from lodger, Eddie Yeats. Their mortgage was refused as Eddie would not commit himself to lodging with the Ogdens for 25 years and their joint incomes were not enough to secure the loan. Hilda was furious and retorted to Stan: 'Any other woman's husband'd get a mortgage on his own wages but not you! It's not because you're self-employed, it's 'cos you earn nowt. An' you know why you earn nowt? 'Cos you do nowt!'

Stan and Hilda's only option was to take their house off the market but then a couple called the Bells came round and offered them £8,000 for the house with an £800 deposit. Tempted by the thought of the money Stan applied for a council house, and to his surprise was offered one immediately for £10 a week. Their problems seemed to be over until Hilda discovered the house was on one of the roughest estates in the area. They rejected the Bells' offer and again stayed on at Number 13. Annoyed and frustrated, Hilda screamed at Stan: 'Stuck in this dump! Stuck here for the rest of us rotten lives!'

Hilda's plan in late 1981 to sell Number 13 and buy a smart, modern house upset Stan who did not really want to move far from the Rovers

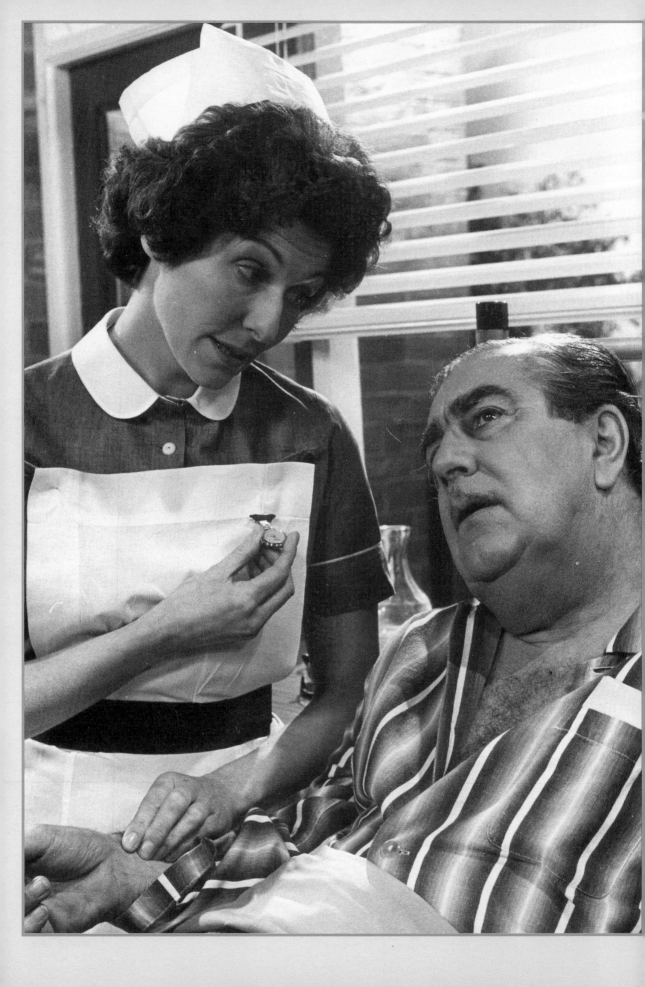

Hilda had a nasty fright about Stan's health in the mid 1970s when he fell off a ladder and collapsed in the street when out on one of his window cleaning rounds. The doctor told him to rest, but he still complained of feeling giddy. Hilda had heard too many complaints about his bad back in the past and she refused to listen. But when Stan told her he was being sent for a check-up at the local hospital she realised he really could be ill and might never come home. He was diagnosed as suffering from Otitis media, a disease which disturbed his balance, and also had anaemia. Hilda felt so guilty – she nursed him night and day and even took on his window cleaning so that he wouldn't lose his customers.

Exhausted by looking after Stan, Hilda went to the doctor herself to get a tonic to revive her. The doctor was surprised to hear that she was still nursing Stan as he had been signed off as fit for work the previous week. At the end of her tether Hilda accosted Stan in the Rovers, threw his window cleaning

Stan's health

Hilda was concerned about Stan's health when he was admitted into hospital for tests, which diagnosed a balance problem (opposite). Back at home, Hilda enjoyed Stan's discomfort as he had to endure several injections in his backside (below)

bucket at him, and shouted: 'You're a louse Stan Ogden. A big, fat nowt-a-pound louse. Lettin' me wear miself to a frazzle. While you sit on yer backside pretendin' to be ill. An when I get you home I'm going to muder you. That's after I've turned ye inside out and shook 'ands with your rotten liver!'

Stan's work record didn't improve and he still continued to take days off at every opportunity blaming his weak back. Poor Hilda never took any time off from her cleaning work at the Rovers or her new evening job sweeping up after the machinists at Baldwin's Casuals. She had no money of her own as she was always supporting Stan and one incident in 1976 finally broke her heart. She had worn a tattered old mac for ten years and had given up on Stan's promises to buy her a new one. Bet Lynch took it one day for a joke when she was working at the Rovers and gave it to local children who were collecting clothes for their bonfire guy to wear.

Hilda was mortified when she saw the guy wearing her mac – it was the only winter coat she had, but she refused to buy it back from the children as a matter of pride. She decided it was time to treat herself and buy a new mac.

Bet Lynch thought it would be a good joke to give Hilda's mac away to young children looking for clothes for their guy. She had no idea of the humiliation and upset this caused Hilda

Cast out by Hilda's vicious tongue, Stan spent most of November 1976 eating his way through the produce at his brother-in-law's fish and chip shop

Raiding her meagre savings she found that only half was left, Stan had spent the rest. All the years of hurt and anguish spilt out and she told him to get out, saying viciously: 'Look at our rotten married life. Knocked about from pillar t'post. In work, out of work. Dole, dole, rotten dole. You an' yer glass back. Her up Inkerman Street. All that lot out there laughin' at us. You want a laugh. Go an' find Stan Ogden. No trouble at all, makin' a mug of 'im. Oh an' don't miss her who's with him. I'm sick of bein' walked on. I'm sick of bein' the mug round 'ere and I'm sick of you!'

Stan was shocked by her outburst and took her literally and left. The days turned into weeks and in her desperation to find Stan, Hilda got in touch with the police and Salvation Army and hoped for his safe return. Stan meanwhile was totally unconcerned that Hilda might be worrying. He had ended up at brother-in-law's, Norman Crabtree's chip shop on the other side of town. Stan quite happily spent his days eating fish and chips and chatting to Norman's girlfriend, Edie Blundell.

Norman eventually told Hilda of Stan's whereabouts and begged her to take him back as he was fed up having him lazing around his shop. Stan agreed to go back provided Hilda apologised for her angry words. Hilda said he couldn't come back until he apologised to her for not

A second honeymoon

While Hilda dreamed of her pampered night in a luxury hotel (above), *all Stan was interested in was the £25 spending money and taking drinks from the mini bar* (below)

saying where he'd gone. She was happy to wait until Stan got bored and came home, but Eddie Yeats told her that Edie was throwing herself at Stan and performing little services for him. Hilda was infuriated and screamed at Eddie, 'He's never lettin' another woman get 'er 'ands on his underpants!' She marched round to the chip shop and told Edie: 'In future you keep yer mucky paws off my Stanley's underpants! Norman fed up with all the arguing insulted Hilda, and when Stan came to her defence the couple were reconciled and left to go back home, together.

For Hilda, one of the highlights of her marriage was winning a second honeymoon in a competition in 1977. Her slogan: 'Be a mistress as well as a wife and your husband'll still be a boyfriend', won her third prize in the Loving Cup

Shandies competition. Her prize was a night out at a luxurious five-star hotel in Manchester. Hilda made the most of it, she borrowed a negligee from Rita Fairclough and loved the sense of occasion when a chauffeur picked them up to take them to the hotel. While she absorbed the glamorous atmosphere of the hotel, Stan sat down and worked his way through the drinks in their mini bar. Before leaving in the morning Hilda made sure she made the bed and tidied the room to leave a good impression.

As Stan got older his health deteriorated and in the summer of 1984 he was struck down by a mystery illness. He was bedridden for four months and Hilda eventually collapsed with exhaustion from the continuous attention that he needed. Stan was taken into Weatherfield General to give Hilda a rest but she refused the hospital's offer to have him transferred to an old soldier's home and said: 'I'm

Hilda was exhausted from nursing Stan through his mystery illness, but refused to let the doctor send Stan to a convalescent home in November 1984

sure he'd be happier at home. He never sleeps well unless he's in his own bed. I'm sure it 'ould be lovely but we wouldn't be together, would we. An' I know it's work for me when we are but...that's what we got married for. In sickness and in 'ealth. Not in convalescent homes'. Sadly Stan never saw his home again; he died quietly in hospital two days later.

Heartbroken, Hilda kept her grief private, refusing to cry in front of other people. After the funeral she cried alone at home and reflected on the 40 years of ups and downs of married life she and Stan had shared. Smiling to

Stan and Hilda knew that the neighbours thought of them as the comic pair, but as long as they could laugh back, together, it didn't matter

herself she recalled one occasion when they had gone out to a French restaurant. It turned out to be the first and only time. The occasion was to celebrate Hilda receiving her brother Archie's inheritance. Neither of them could understand the French menu and they felt uncomfortable sitting among all the smartly dressed people. After the meal Hilda gave the waiter a ten per cent tip and sipped her creme de menthe in complete happiness. Yet it was Stan who really made the evening. Looking fondly at her he said: 'I wouldn't swap you for any 'o this lot'. Hilda was stunned into silence for a moment as it was the first compliment he had paid her for 20 years, but recovered enough to pat his hand and reply affectionately: 'I can't see this one at next table lettin' you run around in yer vest an' underpants, can you?'

It wasn't a perfect marriage, but they suited each other – they rubbed along together, they fitted.

Oh Stan!

'I know folk laugh at us an' look on us as clowns in this Street, but we've got one thin' in our favour haven't we? There's two of us.'

Stan Ogden to Hilda Ogden

The Ogdens were renowned in Coronation Street for all the unfortunate mishaps they seem to attract so easily. Their neighbours treated them as the local comics, but some of their most worrying and hurtful experiences happened inside Number 13. Stan and Hilda were brought closer together by these shared upsets, but never seemed to learn from their mistakes.

Drinking was Stan's favourite hobby but filling in his pool's coupon every week came a close second. He often had to borrow his stake money from Hilda or he stole it behind her back from the gas money tin. He never seemed to win until one week in 1966 he found that his coupon showed all the winning numbers. He was ecstatic when he calculated what he'd won and said to himself out loud, 'With only nine draws on the coupon. It must be at least 'undred thousand,'undred thousand quid. I think I'll ask 'em to pay me in cash, just to see it all. An' to present the money I'll 'ave Shirley Bassey, Dusty Springfield, Eartha Kitt an' Diana Dors'.

He rushed down to the Rovers Return to buy drinks all round. But on his return Hilda broke the bad news to him that she had just filled out the winning numbers on the coupon to check his entry. Stan didn't take this too well and attacked poor Hilda throwing a chair through their bedroom window in the process. Irma arrived home in time to rescue her mother. Stan's ultimate humiliation came when he received the drinks' bill of £6 18s 6d from the Rovers.

The next time Stan thought he'd won the pools was a few years later. But before he had time to celebrate he discovered that Hilda had forgotten to post his coupon. Ironically when Stan and Hilda finally did win some money it wasn't from the pools but from one of Hilda's premium bonds, which came up some time later. They were soon mentally spending their £500 windfall, but in the end Hilda felt guilty about her outstanding debt to Dave Smith, who'd

The pools upset

Stan mentally spent his pools win in 1966 (below). When Hilda confessed to just filling in the coupon with the winning numbers, he nearly killed her. He also became furious in the early Seventies when Hilda confessed to not posting his pools coupon (left)

Hilda's cocktail party

The year 1971 bought Hilda luck when she won the premium bonds (top). She and Stan splashed out on a cocktail bar (middle), but their cocktail party was ruined because Stan had drunk all the miniatures of spirits (right)

lent her money to fly out to Australia and bring back her widowed daughter the previous year. Reluctantly, she paid him back and they were left with £95, so they treated themselves to a cocktail bar and an electric toothbrush. Trying to impress the neighbours Hilda threw a cocktail party but it was a disaster as she didn't know that Stan had drunk all their spirit miniatures and filled them with cold tea! Stan sold the bar in the end to buy some bottles of drink for that Christmas.

Hilda had always thought she possessed special mystic powers. Ever since she was a young girl she'd wanted to be a clairvoyant and learnt how to read tea leaves and palms from somebody she'd worked for. She often used to say to Stan: 'You know Stan, I wouldn't mind bein' a gipsy in the woods. Jumpin' over the camp fire – be smashin' wouldn't it? Romantic like'.

Stan decided to take advantage of Hilda's talent in the late Sixties and charged half a guinea for a consultation with Madame Hilda. Knowing her predictions were completely false he felt he had to follow them up so people believed in her. When Hilda predicted an 'unpleasant experience' for Annie Walker, Stan let a mouse loose in the Rovers. He was

All the neighbours scoffed at Hilda's mystic powers, but nevertheless they were all keen to have their tea leaves read

Stan set Hilda up as a clairvoyant in 1969, turning their living room into Madame Hilda's tent.

The serving hatch

Stan proved his building prowess by creating a serving hatch at Number 13, although as Elsie Howard pointed out it was much more like a barn door!

stumped at her relevation that Valerie Barlow was to have another child. An interested reporter came to seek an interview with Hilda, but Stan couldn't keep up the charade any longer and admitted that she had no powers.

During his on and off working relationship with Len Fairclough and Ray Langton, Stan became determined to prove to them that he could be a good builder when he tried. To prove his point in 1971 he knocked a hole between the front parlour and living room at Number 13 to make a serving hatch. The hole became enormous but even Stan was impressed by the quality of his work. Hilda felt it became the focal point of the room, only matched by her 'muriel'. She was a bit worried about its position, however, and said to Stan: 'It's like they 'ave at that chippie in Balaclava Street. Between shop an' dining room. They pop your steak pudding and peas through. Only the kitchen's over there. We 'ave our meals 'ere, but serving 'atch is over there. So what do we serve through it?'.

In times of trouble the residents of Coronation Street always banded together and in 1972 they formed a male vigilante committee to catch a peeping Tom who had been spotted by some of the women peering through their bedroom windows from the Weatherfield back alleys. One of the men caught Stan hovering suspiciously in a back alley. Stan proclaimed his innocence saying that like them he was watching out for the peeping Tom as Hilda thought she'd seen him. Nobody believed him as Hilda hadn't reported the incident, and all of Coronation Street turned against both the Ogdens. Hilda never doubted Stan's innocence and said in a fury to her neighbours in the Rovers Return: 'Yer a bunch of

Peeping Tom saga

All the Street accused Stan of being the peeping Tom, after finding him lurking in the back alley. No one would believe his story that he was also on the look out for the culprit. Only Hilda stood by him

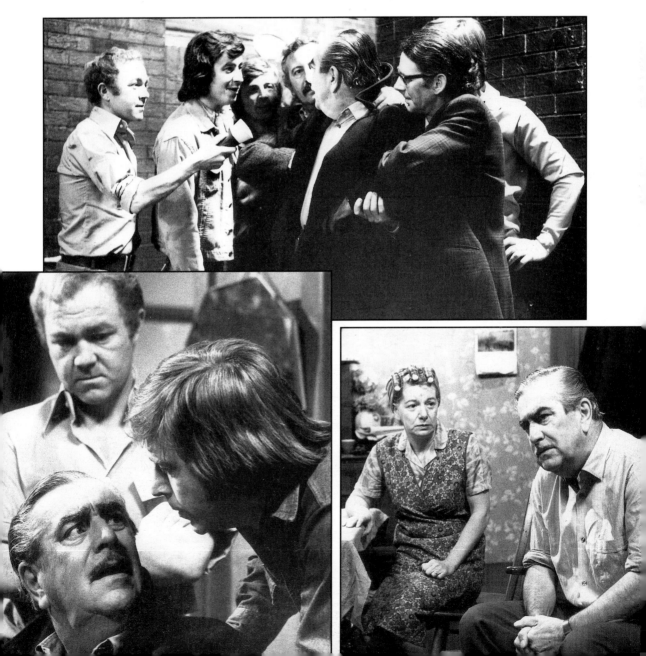

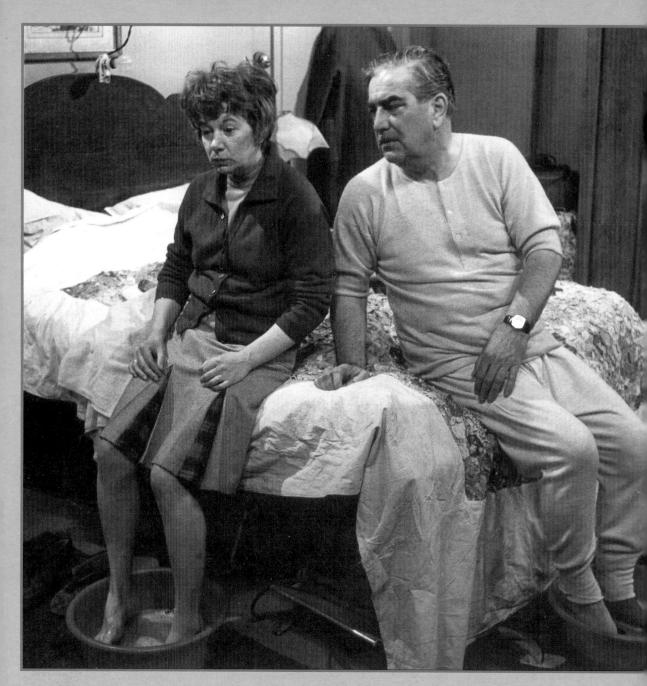

The 1970 walking holiday trip in Yorkshire ended with the Ogdens getting a lift home on a milk float and sore feet for both of them

filthy scum the lot o' you. Scum. Yer none of you fit to lick Stan's boots. A maggot wouldn't stay in 'ere with you lot. You're like a disease'. Stan was exonerated when a man was caught hiding in the alley ways by the police, and he revelled in his neighbour's embarrassment when they had to apologise to him.

The Ogdens hardly ever had a holiday together. They had no money and Stan never wanted to be too far away from his Newton and Ridley beer. Once they went to Yorkshire for a walk, but they hadn't gone far before they lost their map and totally disorientated they ended up in a disused railway station. Tired and hungry they hitched a lift back to the Street on a milk float.

For Hilda's 48th birthday in 1972, Stan promised her a trip to Paris. They got so absorbed in buying their duty free that they missed the plane. Determined not to lose face back home they bought some cheap souvenirs at the airport to give their friends.

Frustrated holidays

The Ogdens got their first passports for their trip to Paris. Having been told not to smile for the photographs they managed to look sombre (insets). Lingering in duty free they managed to miss the flight (below)

The Barbara Cartland party

Hilda was determined to show the Coronation Street residents that she and Stan had style, so she planned a Barbara Cartland party for her 49th birthday (above). Although she did her best to make sure the party followed the correct procedures (opposite), the evening was ruined by the disappearance of Edna Gee (inset) with a mystery man

The following year Hilda's birthday celebration was no more successful. She planned a sophisticated, Barbara Cartland-style party for her friends. To make sure the theme was right Hilda and Stan checked a social etiquette book first, and reading aloud Hilda said: 'Listen to this Stan, Your husband opens the door, shakes 'ands wi' the guests an' suggests that the men put their coats an' 'ats down in the 'all. 'E ses to the women, Would you like to go upstairs'. Stan wasn't impressed and replied: 'I don't need no etiquetty book to tell me that. I've bin sayin' it to 'em for years. Here, one vital point is to say the names of those you introduce clearly. Do give those you introduce a lead: "Mr Basford breeds pekingese"'. To which Hilda replied: 'That's no use, we've not got nobody comin' what breeds pekingese. Greta Pollitt from the fish shop said she might drop in, she's got a 'amster'.

Hilda dressed up to the nines and wore a wig and false eye lashes to the party. She prepared a feast for her guests and when she didn't have any aspic for her hardboiled eggs, she substituted lemon jelly instead thinking nobody would notice. When bookie's clerk, Ted Loftus paid her some attention she was flattered and they spent the evening doing the tango together. The party was spoilt when she found her bedroom door locked and knew Edna Gee was in there with a mystery man. Suspecting it was Stan, Hilda attacked Edna when she reappeared downstairs. When Stan walked back through the front door with some more beer from the Rovers, she burst into tears. The next day Billy Walker owned up to being the mystery man and produced Edna's panties as certain evidence.

During the summer of 1973 Hilda went off to visit her brother Archie and left Stan to fend for himself. Before she left she said to a friend about Stan: 'He's a babe in arms when it comes to looking after 'imself. He really is. I mean you'd think a feller his size with his military experience could at least boil an egg. But can 'e? Can 'e heck. Last egg he tried to boil were that hard he 'ad to ask Wimpeys for an estimate to lift it out of pan!'

While she was away Stan couldn't be bothered to do anything. He neglected the housework, left rotting food around and piles of dirty saucepans filled the kitchen. The first Stan knew that mice had invaded was when Elsie Howard at Number 11 reported their house to the Health Inspector as a health hazard. She feared her home would also be infested with the furry creatures. Hilda arrived home to find the whole house being fumigated and was so ashamed when she discovered only Number 13 had been affected. She bemoaned to Stan: 'Once you've been done, they put y'on the records! You go in't rat book. I've never seen any mice. Not what you'd call mice. Everybody sees one or two. Why's everythin' always happen to us, Stan?'

In 1974 Hilda was bored and frustrated; she felt she was getting old. To improve her spirits, Stan signed her up for what he called a holiday – a cleaning job on a cruise liner. While the holiday-makers sunned themselves by the pool and went off on exotic excursions, Hilda hardly saw the light of day as she worked furiously below deck for the two months she was on board.

Mice infestation

When she returned from a visit to brother Archie in 1973 (opposite, top), Hilda found Number 13 being fumigated to get rid of mice (opposite, middle). Discovering it was Elsie Howard that reported them Hilda attacked her verbally (opposite, bottom)

During the summer of 1974 Hilda was depressed again. Not wanting her to suffer another nervous breakdown, Stan found her an 'easy' cleaning job on a cruise liner

The lodgers

Tommy Deakin and Michael O'Ryan lodged with Stan in Hilda's absence (right). They left behind Dolores the donkey at Number 13, but Hilda soon insisted the animal was moved on her return home in the autumn of 1974 (below)

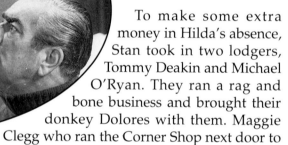

To make some extra money in Hilda's absence, Stan took in two lodgers, Tommy Deakin and Michael O'Ryan. They ran a rag and bone business and brought their donkey Dolores with them. Maggie Clegg who ran the Corner Shop next door to Number 13 saw Dolores and all her manure in Stan's back yard and promptly reported him to the Health Inspector. Tommy and Michael then took Stan for a day out at the races in a chauffeur driven Rolls. Stan couldn't resist driving on the way back to remind him of his old chauffeuring days, halfway home he was stopped by the police and gave a positive breath test. Hilda returned to the fold from the cruise to find the Health Inspector taking the donkey away and a policeman issuing Stan with a driving summons!

When Stan heard that TV detector vans were in the Weatherfield area in the winter of 1976 his immediate thought was to hide their unlicensed rented television. In his rush to put it away he dropped it on the floor and damaged it. It was no consolation when Hilda came back that evening and told Stan that she'd bought a licence. They called out the repair man but he refused to

After breaking their rented TV, Stan had the bright idea of setting fire to it to make it look like an accident. Hilda did not share Stan's confidence in the dishonest scheme

touch it as he could see it had been dropped. Stan then had a brainwave he would set fire to the TV and make it look to another repair man as though the set had caught fire through an electrical fault. He set fire to it with lighter fuel, but it was so badly damaged that the new repair man knew it wasn't a normal fault and presented Stan with a £75 bill – the cost of a new set.

The Ogdens were depressed by the TV incident and were just working out how to pay the bill when they won a competition with a prize of a trolley dash round a delicatessen. Hilda did the shop with Deidre Langton as

Deidre Langton helped Hilda in her trolley dash prize round a local delicatessen. The amount of food they collected nearly bankrupted the owner, who offered Hilda some cash instead

Hilda's inheritance

Archie Crabtree, Hilda's brother, was buried from Number 13 (above right). After the funeral Hilda fought his assistant, April Carter, for his fish and chip shop, which was her rightful inheritance (above)

Stan's fragile back was giving him trouble. Her trolley load came to over £100 of goods much to the manager's dismay. He convinced Stan and Hilda that they'd be much better off with £75 cash and a tin of caviar, which they accepted. They used the £75 to pay back the TV company and settled down happily that evening to a meal of caviar and chips.

Hilda's brother Archie died in 1983 and she thought that she would inherit the fish shop he'd taken over from their brother Norman. Much to her annoyance, Archie's assistant, Avril Carter said the shop should be hers as she was really his common-law wife. Seeing her inheritance disappearing before her eyes, Hilda was determined to prove Avril's story wrong. Her lodger, Eddie Yeats found out through his dustman colleagues that the only night time visitor Avril had was Frank a married man, who worked as a batterer at the chip shop. When Hilda threatened to take Avril to court over the shop, she backed down when Frank said he didn't want their affair made public.

Hilda's victory was shortlived as she was forced to sell the shop to pay off all Archie's debts. She was left with £1,500 so she bought a new carpet and opened a bank account. Stan was fascinated with her new cash card and kept 'borrowing' it to draw out the odd bit of cash to spend on beer and the horses. When Hilda received her next bank statement she saw that her inheritance had dwindled to almost nothing.

After Hilda decided that all their bad luck was down to living at Number 13, Stan changed the door number to Number 12a

To change their never ending run of bad luck, Hilda and Stan bought some new numbers, 12A, from Woolworth's to put on their door in the late Seventies. Hilda thought the re-vamped door looked much better but when they tried to go back in they found they were locked out. Stan had to smash a window to get at their keys, but it was not before their delicious roasting leg of lamb had burnt to a cinder. As they went in to eat their charred food Hilda was heard to mutter: 'Well Stanley, that's another fine mess you've got me into!'

For once the couple had luck on their side when after one of Stan's mishaps they took on Weatherfield district council. Stan had tripped on a loose paving stone and injured his toe in early 1984, and naturally he had to stay off work for a week. Hilda decided to sue the council and made a bed for Stan in the living room to make the injury look worse. She rang up the local newspaper to get some good editorial coverage saying to them: 'His toe's the size of a tennis ball and black as a prune'.

The Recorder took the incident seriously and printed a blown-up photograph of Stan's toe on its front page, much to their neighbours' consternation. Hilda sent a copy to their son Trevor, knowing that he'd like another picture of his dad. The Council was forced to take notice of the case and the Ogdens happily agreed to settle for £200 damages out of court. Hilda was proud of their victory, it wasn't many times in all their years of frustration and bad luck together that she and Stan had, for once, come out on top.

Enterprising Eddie

'I know he's been a wrong 'un and there's lots round 'ere calls 'im. But
he's never 'ad a lot of family. And he's a good mate of mine. So I say yes.
If he wants to move in, lets have 'im...an' if he gets up to 'is old tricks we
can kick 'im out can't we?

Stan Ogden to Hilda Ogden

Edward Timothy Yeats, known as Eddie, came into the
Ogdens lives in 1975. He was an ex-con and had
stayed with Minnie Caldwell at Number 5 when he'd
first come to Weatherfield on parole at Christmas 1974. When
he'd finished his six month prison sentence at Walton jail he
came back to the Street.

Stan Ogden met Eddie in the Rovers Return, where they
found they could match each other, drink for drink. They
became mates and when Eddie heard that Stan was signed off
sick he offered to help Hilda do his window cleaning round.
Eddie and Hilda hit it off straightaway as he appreciated the

*Stan and Hilda soon took
Eddie Yeats to their
hearts and treated him as
their own son*

hard life she had. Out on the round one day he commented: 'It's rough on you, isn't it, flower. You allus get the sharp end o' the stick. Still I s'ppose you come to get used to it, married to a bloke like Stan'. Hilda felt she had a true ally and replied: 'Yer very sympathetic Eddie. It's not many as appreciates me problems'.

When Stan was better he kept Eddie on as his assistant. All went well until Eddie got up to his old tricks and started to case houses that were worth burgling for a friend. After a spate of thefts on one of their rounds, Eddie was arrested for handling stolen goods and sent down to Strangeways prison for a few months.

Eddie wormed his way into the Ogdens lives with his amusing wit and his quick surefire replies

O n his release in the summer of 1976 Eddie moved in as a lodger with ex-con Monkey Gibbons. He didn't get on with his domineering wife, and on renewing his friendship with Stan and Hilda he kept trying to convince them he should move into their spare room. He chose the wrong moment to push the point with Hilda as she and Stan weren't getting on and Stan had moved out. Hilda was worried where Stan was and said to Eddie: 'You can't stay here Eddie, not while Stan's away. People might talk.

Eddie nursed the Ogdens through a bout of flu in 1980 to prove that he'd make a good lodger and could be relied upon in times of crisis

Different when Stan's 'ere but a woman has to protect 'er good name'.

Eddie wouldn't give up and when he found Stan staying with his brother-in-law, Norman, he got him to come home hoping Hilda would relent. But she was insistent: It's not summat you've done. But me an' Stan's kismetted to wind us way through life together. Alone, – without you'.

After much pestering from Hilda, Eddie and Stan agreed to decorate the living room for her later that year. They had papered all the room except one wall when they run out of the cut-price wallpaper that Eddie had bought from a friend. Hilda refused to have non-matching paper on the last wall but was won over by Eddie's convincing suggestion of a scenic vista: 'You see, it gives you what they call a muriel. It's your muriel feature, scenic panorama, contrast wall. Dead trendy. Latest there is'. To their neighbour's amusement Eddie papered the fourth wall with a landscape scene.

Stan instantly liked it and said: 'Puts you in mind of round Garstand...up past Chorley and all round that way'. Hilda thought the mural would be a step up the social ladder and commented: 'Annie Walker's never had one of them muriel walls, that I do know. Go on I think it'll suit us very nicely will that. It'll add a real vocal point to us room will that'.

The precious 'muriel'

Eddie convinced Hilda that she needed a papered, mural scene after he had run out of matching wallpaper (left). The mural she chose was ruined by Suzie Birchall's chimney cleaning (below)

Standing next to the finished backdrop Hilda could see herself as Julie Andrews and regularly used to sing to Stan: 'The hills are alive with the sound of music'. Her precious ornamental plaster ducks fitted in perfectly as they seemed to fly in gracefully over the mountain scene.

Hilda's delight in her 'muriel' was ruined the following year by her next door neighbours. Suzie Birchall, who lodged with Elsie Tanner at Number 11, was trying to do Elsie a favour by cleaning out her chimney by dropping a brick on a string down it. In her haste she dropped it down Number 13's chimney by mistake and soot spilled out into the Ogdens' living room. Stan was having his dinner at the time and getting up to investigate he took his plate to the fireplace, Suzie dropped the brick a second time and Stan and his meal were covered in soot. Hilda came back into the room, saw the sorry scene and exclaimed: 'Stan! What 'ave you been doin'! Look at me muriel, mi mountains 'ave turned into a slag heap'.

The mural was virtually washed away about a year later when Hilda forced Stan to have a bath every night, rather than his usual four a year, to justify the water rates. Stan

Eddie put the idea to Stan that they could use Hilda's machine to financial advantage

didn't agree with too much washing and said to Hilda: 'Too many baths aren't good for you. They're weakenin'. But Hilda was adamant and replied 'If cleanliness is next to godliness I'll make an angel out o' you before I've done!' On the first night Stan fell asleep in the bath and the water overflowed and ruined the wallpaper and mural below.

Hilda was almost in tears, but was determined the mural should be replaced with another scene, saying to Stan: 'Course another muriel. Though I think we might have a change of view. I've gone off pasturised scenes. I think I'd like a seascape this time. So long as me ducks feel at home'. She bought a paper with a sea view and Stan complained, to no avail, that the waves made him feel seasick.

When Hilda bought an old washing machine for £20 in 1977, Eddie and Stan thought of a money earning scheme to put it to good use. They took in washing for Hilda to do, but were rather put out when she refused to get involved. She relented in the end after Ruby Green's bag of washing had remained untouched for two weeks. After washing and drying all the clothes, she spent three hours ironing them all and putting them back in the bag. When Eddie and Stan came back that night they thought the washing still hadn't been done and put it through the machine again. Hilda came back to find Stan ironing the clothes again and when he said they didn't know she'd washed and ironed them, Hilda screamed at them: 'You couldn't tell! You couldn't

Ruby Green came to demand her washing back but Hilda refused to touch it, saying: 'you don't know where it's been!'

tell! After I'd washed it and rinsed it and wrung it out and dried it and ironed it. You couldn't tell?'

Eddie and Stan were always putting their heads together to come up with some money making schemes, but very few succeeded. In the mid-Seventies they bought an Alsation dog called Fury and rented it out to Len Fairclough as a guard dog. The next month Len was broken into and the thieves got away with £200 worth of copper piping and took the amiable Fury as well!

Thinking there was money to be made in cleaning larger windows, Eddie and Stan offered to clean the stained glass windows of St Margaret's, a local church, in 1978. Hours later they went to see the vicar who thanked them profusely for their generous charity. The following year Eddie bought an ice cream van and sold beer with the ice creams on

Fury the Alsatian was bought by Eddie and Stan in 1975. His friendly nature made him useless as a guard dog

61

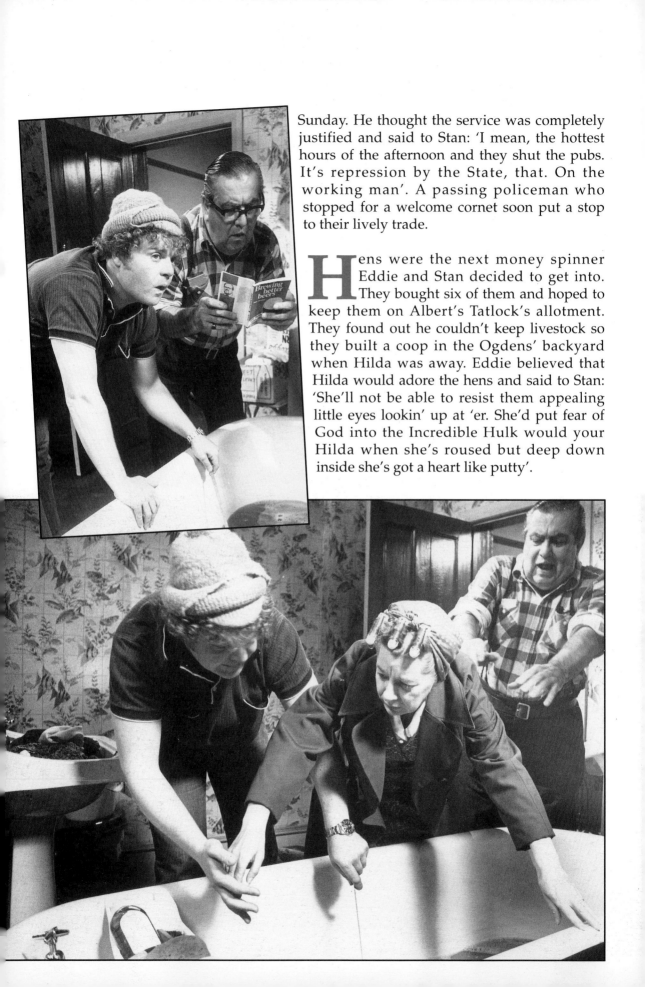

Sunday. He thought the service was completely justified and said to Stan: 'I mean, the hottest hours of the afternoon and they shut the pubs. It's repression by the State, that. On the working man'. A passing policeman who stopped for a welcome cornet soon put a stop to their lively trade.

Hens were the next money spinner Eddie and Stan decided to get into. They bought six of them and hoped to keep them on Albert's Tatlock's allotment. They found out he couldn't keep livestock so they built a coop in the Ogdens' backyard when Hilda was away. Eddie believed that Hilda would adore the hens and said to Stan: 'She'll not be able to resist them appealing little eyes lookin' up at 'er. She'd put fear of God into the Incredible Hulk would your Hilda when she's roused but deep down inside she's got a heart like putty'.

Money spinners

Eddie and Stan tried brewing beer when it was rationed at the Rovers because of a strike. Hilda pulled out the plug because she thought it was illegal (opposite). Finding Hilda the hen standing on the kitchen table (left) should have been no surprise to Hilda; she'd already experienced a houseful of mice and a donkey in the back yard. Stan's birthday in May 1980 was spoilt by little Hilda being served up as the main course of his special dinner (below)

Hilda finally allowed Eddie to move in as their lodger in early 1980 when he took a well-paid job as a dustman

The washing incident

Eddie mistook the Ogdens' laundry for rubbish and put it in the bin making Stan take the household rubbish to the laundrette (inset). The washing ended up on the main rubbish tip, but it was never found (below)

Hilda agreed to the hens staying providing they laid regularly. Worried that they were not laying enough Eddie bought some extra eggs from the Corner Shop to put in their coop. When Hilda found out she demanded that the hens were killed, but when she cooked her namesake, Hilda, for Stan's birthday dinner none of them had the heart to eat her. Stan was quite upset and said: 'I'm not hacking the poor thing to bits. I were fond of that bird. And it were fond of me. She used to come running up t'me y'know. I'm havin' none. I'd sooner starve'.

Eddie finally wheedled his way into lodging at Number 13 in 1980 when he became a dustman. Hilda was impressed by his salary of £60 a week and approved of

Eddie said goodbye to his friends at Number 13 after the Ogdens' 40th wedding anniversary party in December 1983. His wife Marion was also sorry to say goodbye to Stan and Hilda

the idea of having three professional cleaners in the house. She made only one condition to Eddie: 'You pay the rent to me…not Stanley'. He nearly got thrown out not long afterwards when Hilda left a black bag full of washing by the door to go to the launderette. Eddie mistook it for the rubbish bag and put it in the bin, letting Stan take the rubbish to the launderette. They all spent April Fool's day 1981 searching the rubbish tip for the washing – it wasn't found.

Love blossomed for Eddie when he became a CB radio fanatic, calling himself 'Slim Jim' he made contact with 'Stardust Lil', who turned out to be Marion Willis, a florist. Early on in the relationship Eddie nearly lost Hilda's job cleaning Mike Baldwin's flat. Trying to impress Marion he borrowed the keys and took her to the flat, pretending he was a successful businessman. When Mike found out about the deception he agreed not to go to the police on condition that Eddie told Marion the truth about himself. She was relieved as she wasn't really happy going out with someone with lots of money.

Eddie even allowed the Rovers' barman, Fred Gee to insult him about his lowly job in front of Marion when Fred exclaimed: 'Businessman? Him? Not unless they're givin' out pin-striped overalls for bin collecting he's not. An' he's in lodgin's. An the only way he got them were when mice moved out 'cause it weren't good enough for 'em!'

Eddie and Marion had many ups and down in their romance but at last they were married in October 1983. Hilda was proud to act as mother of the groom but was sad when her adopted son and his new wife decided to leave the Street for good to go and live in Bury.

Workshy Oggie

'Being unskilled is the only skill you've got! Me Mam's keepin' you financially, I'm keepin' you financially - and Stanley Ogden's doing very nicely thank you.'

Irma Ogden to Stan Ogden

Stan Ogden could never stay in one job for very long, some lasted weeks, some years, others only days. It wasn't always his well-known laziness that lost him work; some of his inspired schemes just backfired on him. Stan in fact still holds the record, ten years after his death, as the person who had the most jobs in Coronation Street.

One of Stan's longest jobs was working as a long-distance lorry driver. He ended up being sacked by Garston Lorries as he had been caught speeding several times. Stan did not tell Hilda and convinced her he was coming back home permanently to see more of her and the family. His first job back in the Street was replacing Harry Hewitt as chauffeur to the chairman at Amalgamated Steel. He felt very grand

Whether in or out of work, Stan Ogden could always be found every lunchtime propping up the Rovers' bar

Hilda was proud of Stan when he took the chauffeur's job at Amalgamated Steel in 1964. She had always liked him in uniform

driving the company Rolls Royce around and said to Hilda: 'It's a terrifying thought, driving a Rolls; one false move and there's 5,000 knicker gone down't drain'. Bad luck caught up with him when he gave some of the neighbours a ride. Minnie Caldwell's hat pin tore the upholstery and Charlie Moffit's greyhound relieved itself in the car. His employers were furious about the damaged car and he was sacked.

Bored with searching for proper work, Stan was launched not long afterwards on the wrestling world by Minnie Caldwell's lodger, Tickler Murphy. He was a wrestling manager, who thought Stan's large bulk could be put to better use. Stan called himself 'Ogden the Terrible' and

Ogden the Terrible

Giant Ian Campbell soon forced Stan to submit in the wrestling ring (below). Stan's trainer, Tickler, had tried to gee Stan up for battle (right), but failed

used the Mission Hall for training. The Mission caretaker Ena Sharples saw potential money in Stan and demanded ten per cent of his earnings. Stan felt very nervous before his first fight and Tickler tried hard to reassure him: 'I've been doin' a bit of research on this Campbell fellow. He's won a lot o' his bouts on a submission so if he puts the Indian death lock on ye, there's only two things ye can do. Either submit or 'ave yer leg broken. The choice is yours'.

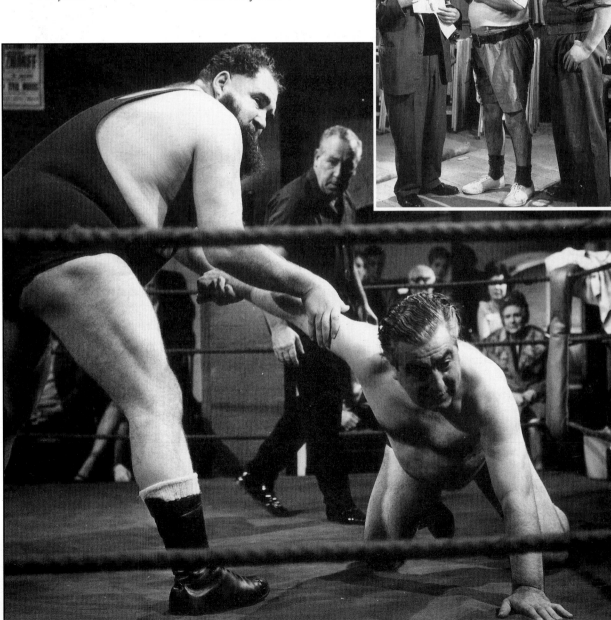

The fight was Stan's first and last as his opponent, giant Ian Campbell, rapidly threw him out of the ring and he landed on Hilda's lap. After paying everyone off he was only left with 30 shillings and decided to find a better paid job.

With Christmas fast approaching the same year, Stan applied to be Father Christmas at Shuttleworth's department store. While he was working there he went into partnership with Charlie Moffit collecting waste paper from the surrounding area. Hilda grew tired of having piles of paper around and in frustration said to Stan: 'You've turned me kitchen int' a rubbish tip!'. Finally she could stand it no more and behind his back she sold it all to a paper merchant for below the market price.

Stan turned Number 13 into a refuge centre for waste paper when he went into business with Charlie Moffit. Hilda could not believe her eyes at the sight of all the paper

Stan the milkman

Stan enjoyed having his afternoons free when he worked as a milkman in February 1966 (above). He found rising at dawn no problem when he worked out a proper system with his alarm clock (above right)

Finishing work at noon seemed extremely appealing to Stan so he took a job at Stebbins Dairy in the February of the next year. He only discovered afterwards that he had to start at 4am. His elaborate alarm clock irritated Hilda and woke up everyone in the Street except him! Trying to make extra money, Stan bought an ice cream van from a drunk in the Rovers. He then organised his day to do his milk round in the mornings and to sell ice creams in the neighbouring streets in the afternoons. He felt the business was going to be a great success and said enthusiastically to Hilda: 'I've got it made this time, I've a definite feelin' it's comin' this time – and' if I ger it made I shall remember me mates. I'm no fly by night! I remember them that does well by me'.

He liked selling to children but before long he upset the ice cream baroness Rose Bonnetti as he was working on her patch. Rose sent her sons out to see where Stan was operating one weekend and managed to keep ahead of him taking all his business. Stan ended up with £20 of wasted stock. He sold the van to Rose and she employed him as a driver. All went well for a while but Hilda grew suspicious of their 'working' relationship and reported him to the authorities for trading without a licence. Stan was furious at losing the job but was secretly rather touched by Hilda's jealousy.

Christmas 1966 was not a happy time for the Ogdens as Stan was made redundant from the dairy. He claimed £8 10s on the dole and refused to take a mill workers' job as it only paid £9 a week. When he turned down another job, his dole was stopped. Hilda threatened to leave unless he found work so reluctantly he joined Howarth's as a coal shifter in the following February.

Breathing in coal soot fumes and having a bath every night didn't suit Stan and he was relieved when Len Fairclough offered him work as a labourer at his building

Stan made the most of Christmas 1966. He let Irma and David provide the food and Hilda do all the cooking

The coalman

Fed up with having Stan refusing to work and living off her wages, Hilda found him a job as a coalman

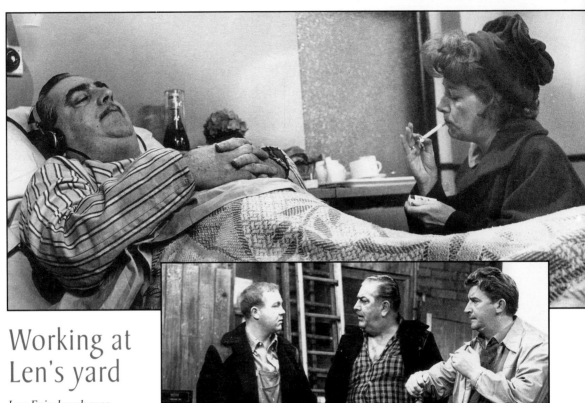

Working at Len's yard

Len Fairclough was Stan's best drinking mate at the Rovers Return. He felt obliged to help him out and employ him at his builder's yard (right) in 1967. However, after only an hour's work Stan put his back out and spent the following week resting in hospital (above)

yard for £14 a week. He managed to put his back out on the first day and spent the rest of the week in hospital!

Back at work, Stan was upset when Len refused to train him as a plumber for a plumbing contract on some new maisonettes locally. He didn't want to mind the Yard so he walked out of Fairclough's and joined the building site constructing the maisonettes on Coronation Street as a labourer. He didn't last long because on the first day he dropped the tea urn on the foreman's foot and scalded his own toe at the same time. Joking around with his work mates as he went upstairs some time later he tripped and dropped a partition down to the first floor narrowly missing some labourers. No more chances were given and he was sacked.

Feeling sorry for Stan, Len Fairclough had him back at the Yard to help out labouring at the maisonettes. As soon as he arrived back at the site, his old work mates downed tools and called a union meeting in the Rovers and demanded his removal. Len stood up and supported Stan saying: 'If you want to accuse a man of bein' thick an' incapable and lazy that's up t'you. But you're judgin' by appearances an' nowt else. Just because a feller's overweight an' carries a big pot-belly doesn't make 'im incompetent'. To keep the peace Len was forced to take Stan off site and left him manning the phone at the Yard.

Stan didn't take too well to being bossed around by Ray Langton at the Yard, and when I-Spy Dwyer offered him a window cleaning round for £45, he bought it and left Fairclough's. To supplement his income Stan became a barman at the Rovers in the evenings, but drank all his wages! When it came to doing the accounts on the window cleaning business, Stan refused to disclose his true earnings to the Inland Revenue, so as a tax dodge he signed the business over to Hilda making himself an employee. Hilda soon got fed up with the amount of time he spent drinking, rather than working, and sold out to Ray Langton, including Stan as part of the package.

Window cleaning fiddle

Signing over the window round to Hilda (left) meant Stan could work for her as an employee. He was stunned when Hilda fed up with him drinking and not working sold the business, with Stan, to Ray Langton (below)

Stan's photo skills

Stan saw a great future on the streets as a photographer with the help of monkey, Marlon. Unfortunately Marlon escaped and bit Dave Smith. This 1969 venture only lasted a week

S tan did not earn a fortune working for taskmaster Ray, and to bring in some extra money, he became a street photographer. He worked for Ernest Bishop and managed to borrow a monkey, Marlon, from one of Len's old girlfriends. He then rode round on his bike trying to persuade people to have their photograph taken with the pet. He complained to Hilda at the time that there was a strange smell following him about to which she replied: 'If ye will run around wi' a gorilla you can expect a strong pong of summat'. The venture ended when Marlon took a dislike to bookie Dave Smith and bit him.

To make matters worse, Stan's bike was flattened by a steam roller. He was really upset at first but looking at the squashed wheels and frame he was inspired to make a scrap

The sculptor

The autumn of 1968 found Stan turning Number 13 into a scrap yard as he turned his hand to metal sculpture. Hilda couldn't believe the public awe at Stan's creations

sculpture, welding his bike bits to other metal sections. His art caused Emily Nugent to comment to Hilda: 'With all due deference Mrs Ogden, Mr Ogden has always been somethin' of a primitive. In his every day to day life. An' now he's found the means to express 'imself. By primitive means. Drain pipes and such'. Stan enjoyed was astounded when a gallery owner agreed to give him a solo exhibition. However, he didn't take care of his priceless works of art and they were removed by the bin men.

On a Street outing to Windermere in November 1969 the coach skidded and crashed. Stan broke his arm and made the most of staying off work. Ray grew tired of his extended 'convalescing' and gave him his cards. Forced to look for another job, Stan was taken on at Holmes' Bakery in 1971 as a night watchman.

Stan and Ena

Stan was impressed by Ena's musical talent and sold some of her songs behind her back (above). He was soon out of pocket when Ena demanded that he pay her a cut of all the money he'd made (inset)

Always on the look out to make a fast buck Stan heard Ena Sharples singing one of her own compositions one day some months later. Taking the song Stan contacted Mickie Malone, a local club singer, and pretended the song was his own. Mickie bought the song for £5 and asked Stan for more. He encouraged Ena to write more saying no one liked the first song. When he claimed her next effort, 'Dreaming Time' had also been rejected, Ena grew suspicious. She followed Stan to the club and heard Mickey singing her song. To teach Stan a lesson she gave him 'Onward Christian Soldiers'. Mickie was not impressed.

Stan enjoyed working for the bakery as instead of keeping watch he spent the nights sleeping in his van. Ray Langton got bored of Stan boasting about his easy life and to teach him a lesson in the following spring, he drove the van – with Stan asleep inside – into waste ground. Police found the van the next day and Stan was sacked, once again. When he discovered it was Ray who had played the joke, Stan did not see the funny side and attacked him in the Rovers. Ray felt guilty and promised to have Stan back at Len's Yard, where was now a partner.

The following year Stan gave up being a labourer and

After Ray Langton made Stan lose his cosy job at the bakery in 1972, he trapped him in the ladies' toilet at the Rovers, and then smashed down the door to fight him

returned to lorry driving. He hadn't been driving long before he had a crash in Newcastle and celebrated his 50th birthday in a hospital bed. When he recovered Len and Ray refused to take him back at the Yard as they had given his job to Jerry Booth, so he bought back his window cleaning round from Ray. When Eddie Yeats moved to the area, Stan felt he needed a young man's help and employed him on the round. Eddie did not last long as the police discovered he was using the round as a cover to commit burglaries.

Stan lasted as a window cleaner, on and off, for 10 years. As he got older he found it harder to climb up the ladders and had to concentrate on mainly cleaning people's downstairs' windows

As Stan grew older and his weight increased, he found it harder to climb up his ladder and tried to just clean downstairs' windows. Hilda still demanded her housekeeping, so he borrowed some money from Sid Kippax, the local money lender. The amount with interest soon spiralled to £184, and Hilda found about the debt when Kippax came round and threatened her with the bailiffs. Eddie Yeats rescued them when he offered to buy the round as a going concern for the amount owed and agreed to employ Stan on the round to wash all the downstairs' windows.

Retirement came sooner to Stan than he expected. Planning a trip abroad in 1983 he applied for a passport and discovered from his birth certificate that he was born in 1919 not 1923 and could retire the next year. Stan thought this was marvellous and suggested to Hilda that she should get hold of her certificate and see if they'd miraculously added some years to her age too!

Hilda the Work Horse

'My life's just one long flamin' clean up!'

Hilda Ogden

Not far down the Street from Number 13, where the Ogdens lived stood the Rovers Return public house. During the Ogden family's stay in the Street it was run by Jack Walker, and after his death his wife, Annie took over. Jack was an amiable, easy going character totally different from his haughty and fussy wife who demanded respect and deference from all the customers. Annie Walker employed Hilda as a cleaner at the pub and their relationship was at best friendly and at worst hostile through the many years they worked together. Hilda Ogden was always the epitome of the true char lady, easily recognisable in her familiar, flowery wrap-around pinny with her hair always in curlers and wrapped in a turban.

Stan Ogden, Hilda's husband, spent most of his earnings on drink, so Hilda went to work for Annie in July 1964 shortly after they'd moved into the area. Her daughter Irma also worked there in the evenings as a barmaid. Annie

Annie Walker employed Hilda to help clean the Rovers Return in 1964. For the next 19 years they had very a strong working relationship

78

looked down on Irma's
blatant flirting with the male
customers and disliked the
way she swapped rude
jokes with them. She didn't dare
sack her for fear of upsetting Hilda, who was a
treasure. The day Hilda started work Annie realised she was
worth her weight in gold and later commented to one of her
customers: 'The woman is an absolute saint. Very thorough.
That's something I always admire, thoroughness. Her
financial affairs are quite another matter. A little
thoroughness there wouldn't be misplaced. Her husband
will be in for his beer any minute. Scandalous is the only
word for it'.

Cleaning up one day shortly after she'd started work at
the Rovers, Hilda found £25 in a cigarette packet left lying on
the bar. She went against the house rule to hand everything
in, pocketed the money and bought a two-piece suit with it.
When she discovered it was the day's takings of insurance
man, Charlie Moffitt, a good friend of Stan's, she didn't
know what to do. Irma came to her rescue by lending her the
money to repay Charlie in full. Hilda swore to her daughter
that she'd never be tempted again.

The
Rovers
Return

*Hilda was always on hand
in a crisis, such as a burst
pipe* (top left) *and was
regarded as a treasure by
her employer, Annie.
Finding £25 at the pub,
Hilda splashed out on a
two piece* (top right)
*before discovering the
money belonged to
insurance man, Charlie
Moffitt* (bottom)

After a run in with fellow cleaner, Bessie Proctor, Hilda was made senior cleaner at The Capricorn Club in 1973

After working at the betting shop, Hilda took a job as a cleaner at Alan Howard's hair salon. She longed for the chance to become a hair stylist, but manageress Elsie Tanner just couldn't take her ambition seriously

After working for Annie Walker for several years, Hilda was infuriated when all the bar staff received a rise of £1 but she received nothing. She tried housekeeping for a while but it didn't work out so she decided to take on more cleaning work. In 1972 she did some work for Benny Lewis who owned the betting shop and the apartment above. She became head cleaner at his club 'The Capricorn', which he named after Hilda picked a

star sign. Alan Howard, the club's joint owner, sacked her when she spread the rumour that he was having an affair with the club's singer, Rita Littlewood.

Stan Ogden was the Rovers best customer. In the 20 years he spent drinking there he managed to spend more than three times the money that Hilda earned there. In fact, in 1975 the pub's brewery, Newton & Ridley, had him photographed for their in-house magazine as his continuous attendance had become a record in Weatherfield. One of the barmaids worked out that he'd drunk 2,000 pints a year and joked: 'Just imagine that. That river of ale. Washin' past them tonsils'.

A year later, Stan nearly lost Hilda her job. To earn some free drinks he helped neighbour Albert Tatlock carry some beer crates down to the Rovers' cellar. On closing, Annie locked the cellar door, not realising they were still in there. Forced to spend the night down there, they drank beer to keep warm. Hilda was worried sick about Stan and stayed up all night waiting for him to come home. In the morning Annie heard Albert and Stan's drunken voices and on letting them out promptly banned them from the pub. When all the residents heard the story they backed the hapless pair and made Annie let them return.

A night in the cellar

After being locked in, Albert and Stan kept warm in the cellar by drinking the beer (top left). *When she found them in the morning, Annie banned them both from the pub* (above)

Baldwin's Casuals

Hilda didn't like to see the sewing machines at Baldwin's standing idle so she used them to make her curtains (inset). When she was sacked by Mike Baldwin in 1979 her work mates stood by her and called a strike (above)

Working at Baldwin's Casuals a few years later suited Hilda. She went in each evening to sweep up after the machinists. The idle sewing machines were hard to resist and she used them to run up some curtains for herself. Unfortunately, Mike Baldwin found out and stopped this extra activity. In 1979 Hilda complained to him about her cleaning materials which were falling apart. She asked him for a new brush head saying: 'Brain surgeons 'ave got the right stuff, an' doctors an' people. What 'ave I got? A bald mop and a sick brush'. Mike retaliated by accusing her of vandalising the brush on purpose and sacked her. Hilda was pleasantly surprised when her work mates went out on strike in support of her. But as the strike continued for over a week she soon grew tired of picketing and got a better paid job cleaning at the local abattoir. She wasn't so pleased when Mike agreed to reinstate her and she had to forfeit her increased wages.

She was forced to leave the factory in 1980 after she fell out with one of the machinists, Vera Duckworth. Vera was always picking on Hilda and one day she had had enough. Taking Vera's pools coupon she filled that week's winning pool's score onto her coupon. Forgetting that she hadn't filled it in, Vera and her work mates celebrated a big win and went out and bought themselves fur coats. Hilda realised the joke had got out of hand and nervously told Mike the whole story. He told the machinists what had happened and left it to them how to punish Hilda. They were adamant that she should go so Hilda was given her cards.

Mike didn't really want to lose Hilda and told her bluntly: 'Hilda, that lot across the road have got memories that make elephants look like absent-minded professors. They don't trust you, Hilda. They'll swear blind I've put you in there to spy on 'em and that kind of aggro I do not want!' Instead he employed her in 1981 to clean his luxury flat, which was situated near by. Once she had learnt how to switch the burglar alarm off, Hilda liked having the flat to herself. She was offended when Mike moved in his girlfriend, Maggie Dunlop, a few months later and made her views very clear: 'You can like somebody without livin' over brush with 'em If everybody did that there wouldn't be a brush left in shops'. She refused to work in a ''ouse of sin' but relented when Mike gave her a £1 a week rise.

Vera celebrated a big pools win in 1980 and bought a fur coat (inset). *She was furious when Hilda confessed that she'd filled in the coupon* (below)

Hilda decided she needed a treat in December 1980 and appointed Brenda Palin as her personal cleaner for a couple of weeks, so that she could come home and put her feet up

Hilda cleaned and worked for many people over the years and there came a point in the early 1980s when she decided she needed a treat. She saved up her wages and employed her own cleaner, a Mrs Palin, for two weeks. Stan couldn't understand why on earth she didn't do the cleaning herself as usual and Hilda tried to explain to him: 'For nearly forty years I've bin doin' it meself. Stanley. I've bin comin' 'ome to muck out this pig stye after I've slogged meself for other people. For once I've nowt to do but put me feet up'.

In 1982 Hilda was delighted to learn that she had been appointed cleaner to Dr and Mrs Lowther at Goldenhurst, Bolton Road, Weatherfield. It was a large detached property by the golf course and Hilda revelled in polishing up all the mahogany and oak furniture. She was ashamed when the Lowthers called in on her once at home and discovered Stan lounging around in his vest. Stan was completely unperturbed, especially when he found out that the doctor had been a fellow desert rat. The doctor's wife died in November 1987 and he gave up his practice and moved to Derbyshire soon afterwards. Hilda, now a widow herself, gratefully accepted his offer to go with him as his housekeeper.

When she left Coronation Street, Hilda was touched by the surprise party that was thrown for her by her friends and neighbours. The Rovers Return had dramatically changed since she'd first started working there 23 years earlier. Bet Lynch (now Gilroy) had taken over the pub from Annie Walker and had nearly been killed in a fire caused by faulty electrics. It was Hilda, her longest serving member of staff, she had immediately thought of to open the refurbished pub in 1986. Hilda had felt extremely honoured and had performed the ceremony with immense pride.

The highlight of Hilda's working life was opening the refurbished Rovers Return in September 1986. Her one regret was that Stan wasn't alive to see the ceremony

Life After Stan

'I find it 'ard to make me mind up about things. Stan was the one who made all the decisions in our house. Even if they were't wrong uns sometimes.'

Hilda Ogden

Stanley Isaiah Ogden died on 21 November 1984 in Weatherfield General Hospital after suffering a mystery illness for several months. Hilda received the news by phone at the Corner Shop – they still didn't have their own. Her friends and neighbours rallied round her taking the burden off her shoulders by sorting out all the necessary paper work and organising the funeral. Irma Barlow sent a letter of sympathy from Canada, but didn't come home for the funeral feeling that she didn't owe her father anything. Her brother Trevor came to support his mother but couldn't wait to go home as soon as all the other mourners had left. Hilda was left to weep on her own with her memories, some good, some bad, of the 40 years of volatile married life she and Stan had shared.

Hilda wasn't used to being on her own at Number 13 because some months before Stan died she had briefly taken in young Terry Duckworth as a lodger when he fell out with his parents. He had returned home when his mother Vera made a scene at Number 13 and insulted Hilda in her own home by saying: 'He'd 'ave to be addled to swop his nice comfy home for a dump like this. You've been trying to get yer hooks into another meal ticket since Eddie Yeats packed 'is bags. Cos your Stan doesn't bring in enough to keep a sparrer alive'.

Just over a month after Stan's death Hilda took on a new lodger, Henry Wakefield. He told her at first that he worked at Piccadilly Railway Station in Manchester, but later confessed he was unemployed. He had walked across a picket line at the station to work because he desperately needed the money to look after his dying mother. His work colleagues and neighbours had branded him a blackleg and

had even boycotted his
mother's funeral. Hilda
was moved by his story
and found him a job at
Baldwin's Casuals. Un-
fortunately the machinists
found out his past history and demanded he
should be sacked. Hilda was furious that they should be so
petty minded and she turned vehemently on the factory
girls: 'I've done wi' you lot. Playin' about wi' folk's futures
without a thought. You've denied me my new start, after
Stan. I were really enjoying havin' somebody to do for again.
I felt Ii were startin' to cope again. All gone now in't it!'

She was not disheartened for long as four months later
young mechanic, Kevin Webster came to stay. He lived at
Number 13 for two years, and brought back many of his
lively, young friends to cheer up Hilda. She didn't approve
of his girlfriend, Sally Seddon at first and said pointedly to

Terry Duckworth

*After Stan's death, Hilda
filled the house with young
people (above). Terry
lodged with her briefly,
just before Stan's death,
much to his mother's
annoyance (inset)*

Kevin and Sally

Mechanic Kevin Webster moved into Hilda's spare room in 1985 (right). A year later she relented and let his girlfriend Sally move in (inset)

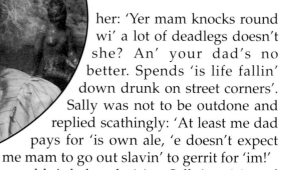

her: 'Yer mam knocks round wi' a lot of deadlegs doesn't she? An' your dad's no better. Spends 'is life fallin' down drunk on street corners'. Sally was not to be outdone and replied scathingly: 'At least me dad pays for 'is own ale, 'e doesn't expect me mam to go out slavin' to gerrit for 'im!' Hilda couldn't help admiring Sally's spirit and when Kevin told her he loved Sally, she tried to change her views on the Seddon family. When Sally's father threw her out she was against her moving in with Kevin and said: 'I have certain standards which I've tried to keep up meself. Though I do understand how 'ard it must be for you. In this godless, wicked world'. She relented and let Sally have the front parlour after she'd met the Seddons and heard that Sally gave all her earnings to her father. She talked frankly to Kevin about Sally, saying: 'I thought her mother was just

common. A loud mouth. But it's obvious what goes on in that house. It's him, the husband. She's frightened to death o' 'im. I don't want Sally to have to go back there. And be scared out of 'er wits. But you behave yourselves whilst yer under my roof. you know what I mean. I don't have to draw no diagrams'.

Determined to keep Sally and Kevin apart from each other at night Hilda placed a metal bucket on the stairs to trip them up if they left their rooms. Her plan failed when she forgot about her own trap, and on venturing out of her room she tripped on the bucket spraining her ankle!

Hilda's attempts to keep the young lovers out of each other's rooms backfired when she fell over her own trap of a metal bucket and sprained her ankle

Life as a widow was not without its romances for Hilda. In 1987 Sally's uncle, Tom Hopwood, a greengrocer came to stay shortly after she and Kevin had got married. Tom got on well with Hilda and came back to visit bringing her presents of vegetables and fruit from his shop. They started to go dancing together and even went on

Hilda was tempted by grocer Tom Hopwood's proposal of marriage. She liked the look of his new bungalow in Formby, but decided that Number 13 held too many memories for her to leave

holiday with some other old-age pensioners. When Tom retired he bought a bungalow in Formby and asked Hilda to join him, as his wife. Hilda seriously considered the offer because Tom was a good, kind man, but in the end she turned him down saying she couldn't leave her home: 'Just about everthin' important, bad or good, great or small, that ever 'appened to me, 'appened round 'ere. All me memories are 'ere'. In her heart she knew that she couldn't marry anyone else after Stan.

At this time Hilda was working for the Lowther's and in the November they sold their house to retire to the country. Hilda was sad to lose them and offered to help them pack. On the night of the 23rd Hilda and Joan Lowther were packing up the silver while Dr Lowther went out to buy them all a Chinese takeaway. Two burglars broke into the house and tried to make off with the silver and some other goods. Hilda caught them in the act and grappled with one of them, trying to wrench back the couple's cherished candlesticks. In the struggle Hilda was pushed backwards and she fell hitting her head on a table. The other burglar tried to stop Mrs Lowther screaming and Dr Lowther arrived home to find his wife had suffered a heart attack and Hilda was unconscious on the floor.

The robbery

The evening Hilda spent helping her employers, the Lowther's, to pack up for the move in November 1987, nearly cost Hilda her life when she wrestled with burglars (above). Recovering from her injuries in hospital she was delighted to receive a visit from her old lodger Eddie Yeats (left)

Hilda came round in the hospital to find out that Mrs Lowther was dead. She was heartbroken but immediately offered some comforting words to Dr Lowther: 'There were things I wished I'd said to Stan. But he knew what I thought about 'im. He knew. An' Mrs Lowther, she knew what ye thought about 'er. I'm quite sure of that'.

Hilda accepted Dr Lowther's job offer, and packed her set of flying ducks before waving goodbye to her muriel

Back home at Number 13, Hilda did not feel safe anymore. The Websters had moved out to live above the shop next door, so she was all alone. She started to become a prisoner in her own home, locking herself in and refusing to answer the door if anyone knocked. She sadly admitted to a friend: I've lived round 'ere all my life. I've never known much but t'back streets. I used to feel safe... I knew there were the rough end like... But since bein' set on. Well, I'm dead scared'.

The future seemed bleak for Hilda, but she hadn't been at home long before Dr Lowther contacted her from his cottage in Derbyshire and asked to come and be his housekeeper. She went up to see his new home and she fell in love with the private, self-contained flat above the garage that he offered her. Hilda readily agreed to work for Dr Lowther as she felt the time was right for her to leave Coronation Street and she felt he needed looking after. Thinking back to the past she said to him: 'I'll be takin' the good memories with me. Me and Stan...and the children, when they were little. But there's other memories I'll be glad to leave behind. As long as I can be a bi' of use to somebody. That's what I like'.

Kevin and Sally Webster wanted a house and agreed to buy Number 13 from Hilda and she left Coronation Street for 'The Nook' on Boxing Day 1987. Her surprise leaving party at the Rovers left her close to tears and she cherished her present of some heated rollers for her hair. As she left Hilda sang, 'Wish me luck as you wave me goodbye', and looked forward to a new and safe life in Derbyshire as a woman of comfortable means.

The residents of Coronation Street gathered in force on Christmas Day 1987 to give Hilda a good send off. She left the Street the next morning, full of memories of all the times she spent in the house where she had lived for 23 years

Amusing Moments

'Disasters seem to follow you about like rain did St Swithin.'Ave you seen state of place? Specially me lovely murial. That snow-capped peak's like the coal man's hat. And me ducks are all crows.'

Hilda Ogden to Stan Ogden

In Christmas 1968 the Ogdens portrayed Widow Twankee and Wishey Washey in the Street's production of Aladdin ▶

▼*During a visit to Woburn Abbey in 1973, Hilda couldn't contemplate cleaning the banqueting hall*

◄ *In October 1969, Hilda and Stan played in a 5-a-side match against the Flying Horse. Hilda unfortunately scored a home goal*

To celebrate his new window round in July 1968, Stan took Hilda to a Chinese restaurant where they ignored the Oriental food and had ◄ *egg and chips*

▼ *Stan and Hilda stopped their wisecracking when they were reunited with their son, Trevor in November 1973*

The Cast

Mike Baldwin	JOHNNY BRIGGS
David Barlow	ALAN ROTHWELL
Irma Barlow	SANDRA GOUGH
Ken Barlow	WILLIAM ROACHE
Val Barlow	ANNE REID
Emily Bishop	EILEEN DERBYSHIRE
Ernie Bishop	STEPHEN HANCOCK
Suzie Birchall	CHERYL MURRAY
Edie Blundell	AVIS BUNNAGE
Rose Bonetti	LILIA KAYE
Minnie Caldwell	MARGOT BRYANT
Ian Campbell	HIMSELF
Avril Carter	JEAN RIMMER
Maggie Clegg	IRENE SUTCLIFFE
Archie Crabtree	JOHN STRATTON
Norman Crabtree	STAN STENNETT
Tommy Deakin	PADDY JOYCE
I Spy Dwyer	ROY BARRACLOUGH
Joe Donnelli	SHANE RIMMER
Vera Duckworth	ELIZABETH DAWN
Terry Duckworth	NIGEL PAVERO
Eddie Duncan	DEL HENNEY
Maggie Dunlop	JILL KERMAN
Len Fairclough	PETER ADAMSON
Greg Flint	BILL NAGY
Fred Gee	FRED FEAST
Edna Gee	MAVIS ROGERSON
Bet Gilroy	JULIE GOODYEAR
Ruby Green	OLGA GRAHAM
Agnes Greenwood	KATHLEEN HELME
George Greenwood	ARTHUR PENTELOW
Top Hopwood	LEW MARTEN

Alan Howard	ALAN BROWNING
Sid Kippax	BRIAN LAWSON
Ray Langton	NEVILLE BUSWELL
Dr Lowther	DAVID CASE
Joan Lowther	JUNE BROUGHTON
Micky Malone	BILL MAYNARD
Charlie Mofitt	GORDON ROLLINGS
Jill Morris	LINDA COOK
Tickler Murphy	PATRICK MCALINNEY
Michael O'Ryan	JIM BARTLEY
Hilda Ogden	JEAN ALEXANDER
Stan Ogden	BERNARD YOUENS
Damien Ogden	NEIL RATCLIFFE
Polly Ogden	MARY TAMM
Trevor Ogden	DON HAWKINS
Brenda Palin	SANDRA VOE
Bessie Proctor	JILL SUMMERS
Alf Roberts	BRYAN MOSLEY
Ena Sharples	VIOLET CARSON
Dave Smith	REGINALD MARSH
Elsie Tanner	PATRICIA PHOENIX
Albert Tatlock	JACK HOWARTH
Henry Wakefield	FINETIME FONTAYNE
Billy Walker	KENNETH FARRINGTON
Annie Walker	DORIS SPEED
Jack Walker	ARTHUR LESLIE
Sally Waterman	VIKKI CHAMBERS
Kevin Webster	MICHAEL LE VELL
Sally Webster	SALLY WHITTAKER
Eddie Yeats	GEOFFREY HUGHES
Marion Yeats	VERONICA DORAN